Alfred's Basic Piano Library

Popular Hits ◆ Level 5

P i a n o

MW01259641

Arranged by Tom Gerou

This series offers Broadway, pop, and movie music arrangements to be used as supplementary pieces for students. Soon after beginning piano study, students can play attractive versions of favorite classics, as well as the best-known popular music of today.

This book is correlated page-by-page with Lesson Book 5 of *Alfred's Basic Piano Library*; pieces should be assigned based on the instructions in the upper-right corner of the title page of each piece in *Popular Hits.* Since the melodies and rhythms of popular music do not always lend themselves to precise grading, you may find that these pieces are sometimes a little longer and more difficult than the corresponding pages in the Lesson Book. The teacher's judgment is the most important factor in deciding when to assign each arrangement.

When the books in the *Popular Hits* series are assigned in conjunction with the Lesson Books, these appealing pieces reinforce new concepts as they are introduced. In addition, the motivation the music provides could not be better. The emotional satisfaction that students receive from mastering each song increases their enthusiasm to begin the next one.

ISBN-10: 1-4706-3960-2
ISBN-13: 978-1-4706-3960-0

Produced by
Alfred Music
P.O. Box 10003
Van Nuys, CA 91410-0003
alfred.com

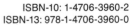

Use with Alfred's Basic Piano Library, Lesson Book 5, after pages 2–3.

City of Stars
(from *La La Land*)

Music by Justin Hurwitz
Lyrics by Benj Pasek & Justin Paul
Arr. by Tom Gerou

Moderate swing tempo

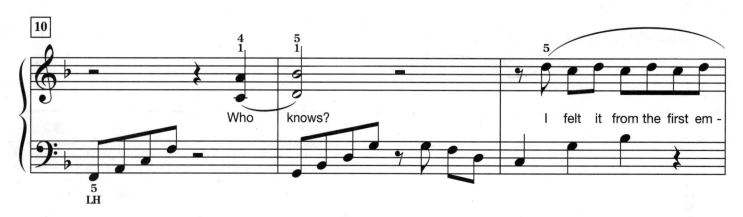

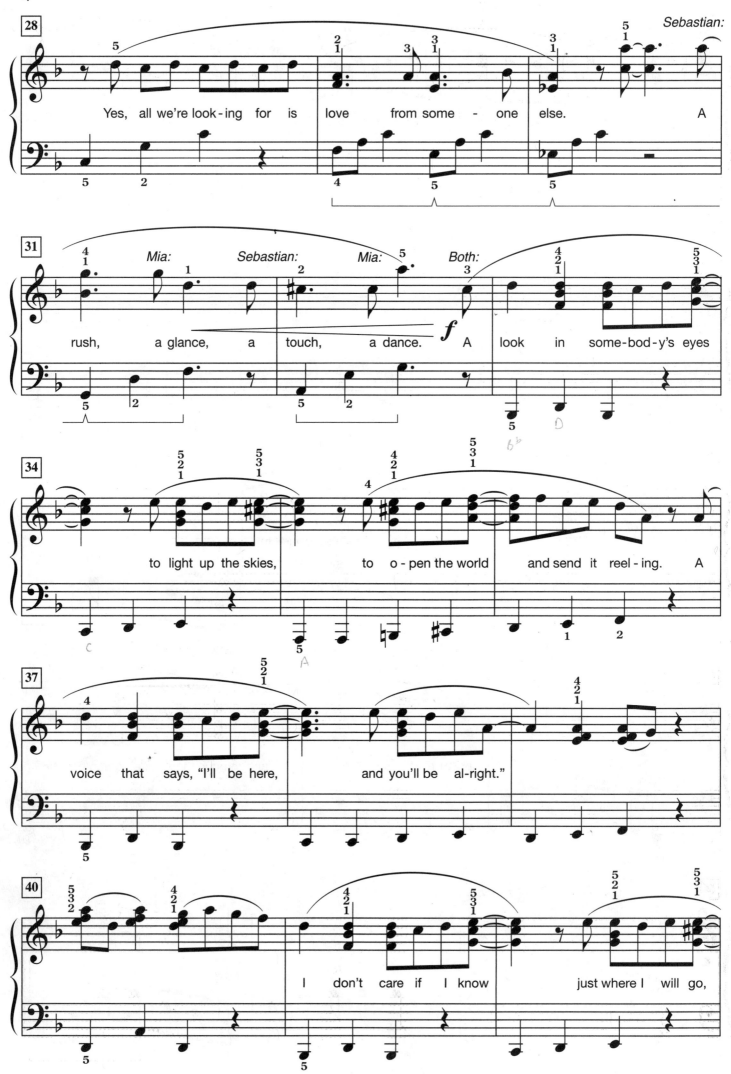

Use after pages 6–7.

The Jetsons
(Main Theme)

Words and Music by
William Hanna, Joseph Barbera and Hoyt Curtin
Arr. by Tom Gerou

Meet George Jet - son!

Jane, his wife.

Daugh - ter Ju - dy.

His boy El - roy.

Ro - sy, the ro - bot maid.

And

Wonder Woman's Wrath
(from *Wonder Woman*)

Use after pages 8–9.

By Rupert Gregson-Williams
Arr. by Tom Gerou

Allegretto

Count: 1 - 2   1 - 2   1   2   3

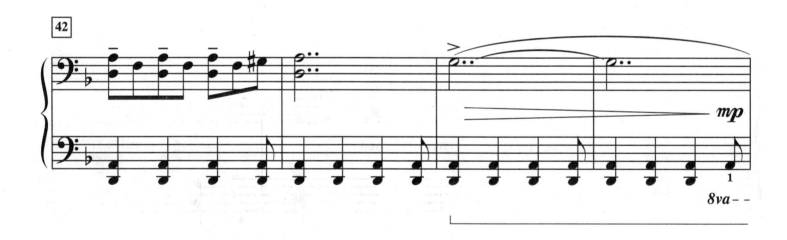

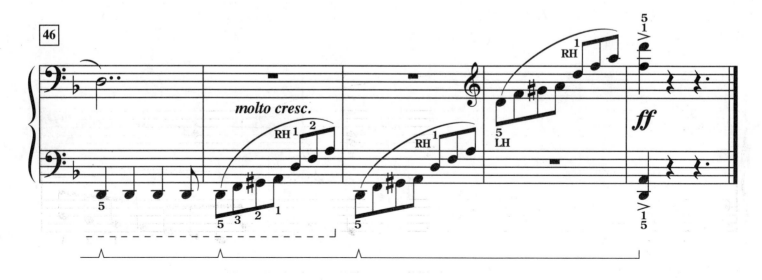

Shut Up and Dance

Words and Music by Ryan McMahon, Benjamin Berger,
Nicholas Petricca, Sean Waugaman, Kevin Ray and Eli Maiman
Arr. by Tom Gerou

Moderate rock tempo

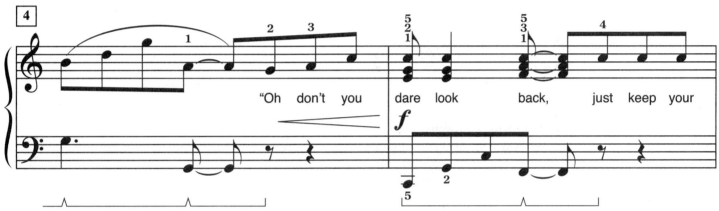

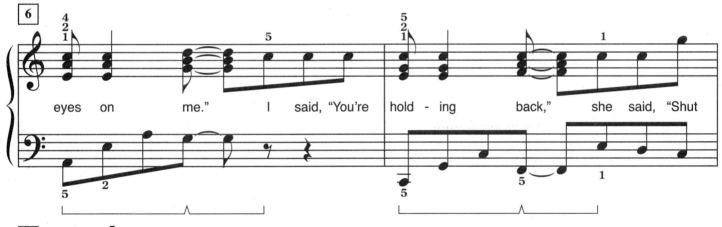

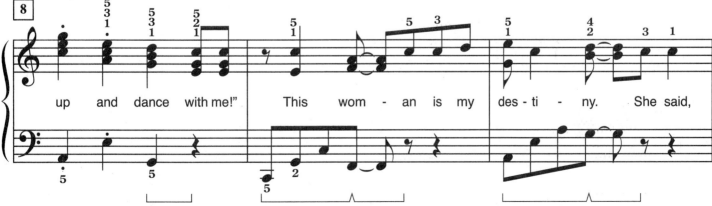

"Ooh, shut up and dance with me!" *mp*

We were

vic - tims of the night, the chem - i - cal, phys - i - cal, kryp-ton - ite,

help - less to the bass and fad - ed light. Oh, we were bound

to get to - geth - er, bound to get to - geth - er.

Use after pages 22–23.

Batman Returns

(from *Batman Returns*)

By Danny Elfman
Arr. by Tom Gerou

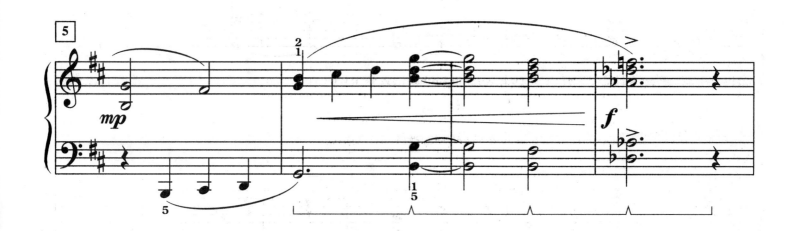

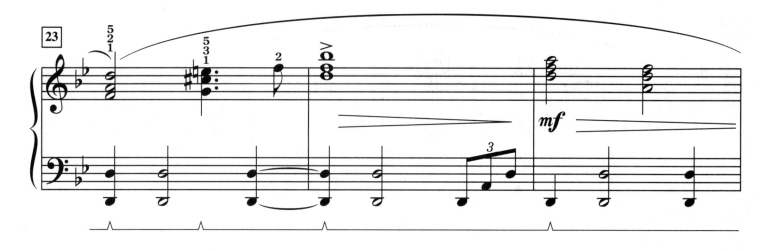

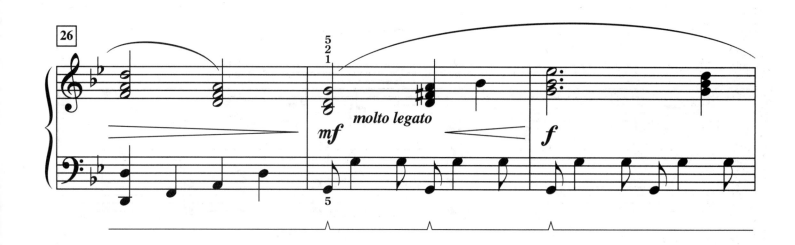

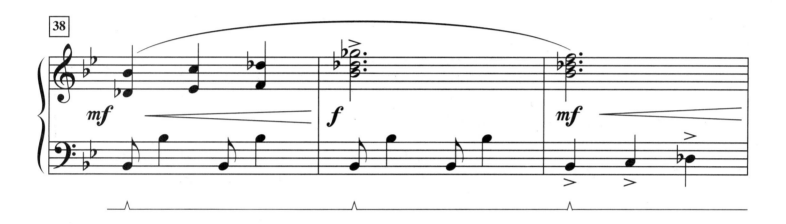

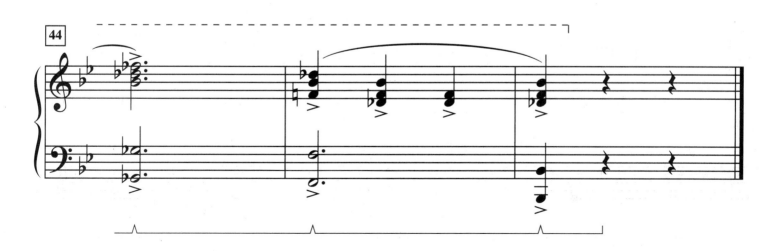

Use after pages 26–27.

Dear Theodosia
(from the Broadway musical *Hamilton*)

Words and Music by Lin-Manuel Miranda
Arr. by Tom Gerou

Allegretto

Dear The - o - do - sia, what to say to you?

You have my eyes. You have your moth - er's name. When you

you knock me out, I fall a - part. And I thought I was so

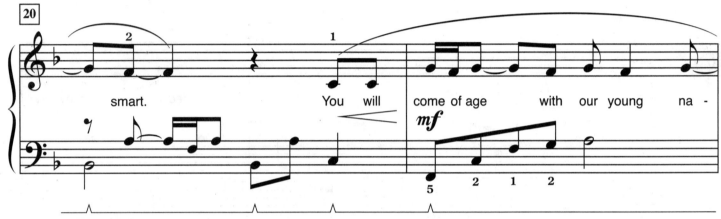

smart. You will come of age with our young na -

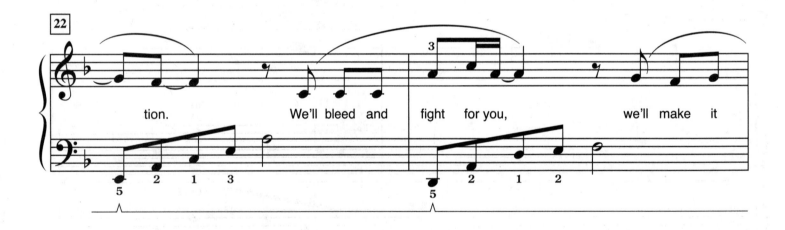

tion. We'll bleed and fight for you, we'll make it

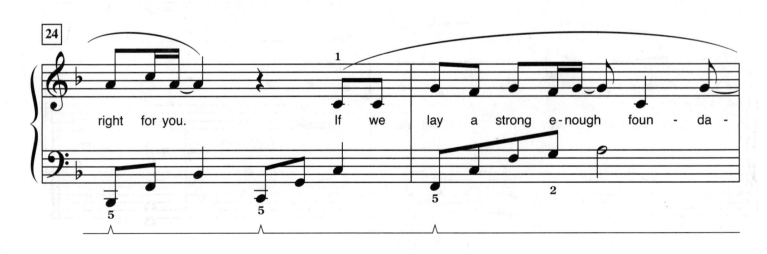

right for you. If we lay a strong e - nough foun - da -

Use after pages 30–31.

Evermore

(from Walt Disney's *Beauty and the Beast*)

Music by Alan Menken
Lyrics by Tim Rice
Arr. by Tom Gerou

Slowly and quietly

I was the one who had it all;

I was the mas-ter of my fate.

I nev-er need-ed an-y-bod-y in my life;

I learned the truth too late. I'll nev-er shake a-way the

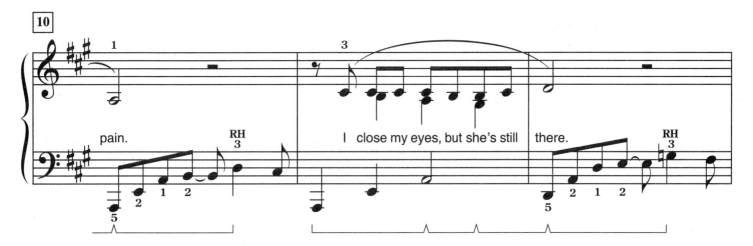

pain. I close my eyes, but she's still there.

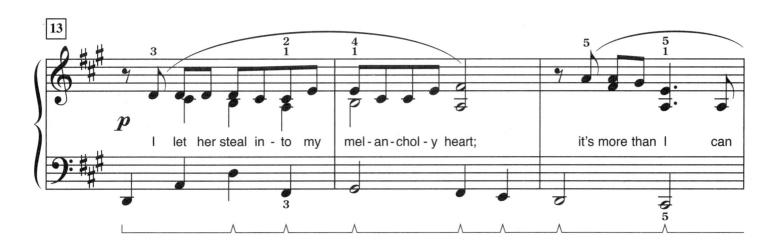

p I let her steal in - to my mel - an - chol - y heart; it's more than I can

With motion

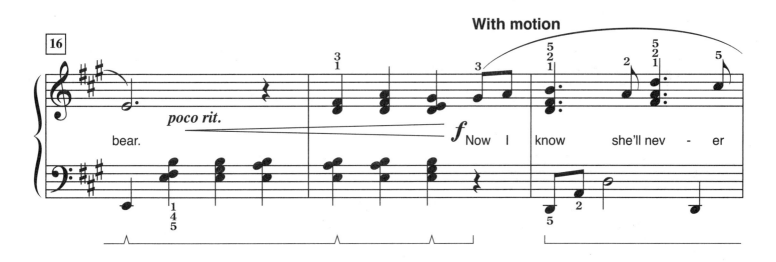

poco rit. bear. *f* Now I know she'll nev - er

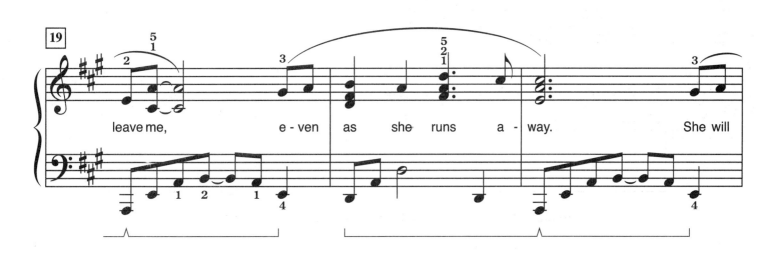

leave me, e - ven as she runs a - way. She will

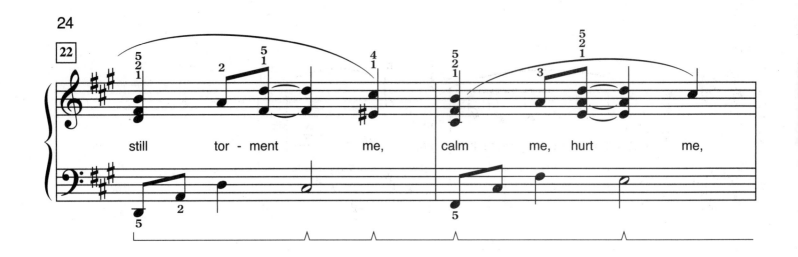

still tor - ment me, calm me, hurt me,

move me, come what may. Wast-ing in my lone - ly

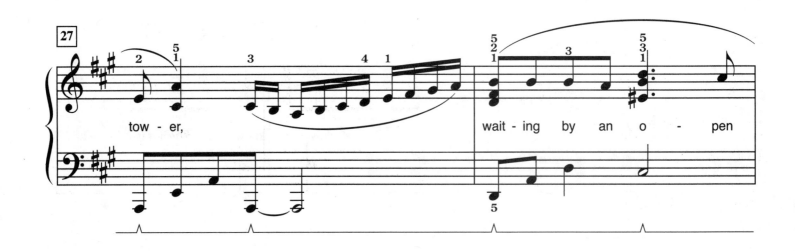

tow - er, wait - ing by an o - pen

door, I'll fool my-self she'll walk right in,

and as the long, long nights be - gin, I'll think of all that might have been, wait - ing here for ev - er - more.

Use after pages 36–37.

Don't Stop Believin'

Words and Music by Jonathan Cain,
Neal Schon and Steve Perry
Arr. by Tom Gerou

Moderate rock tempo

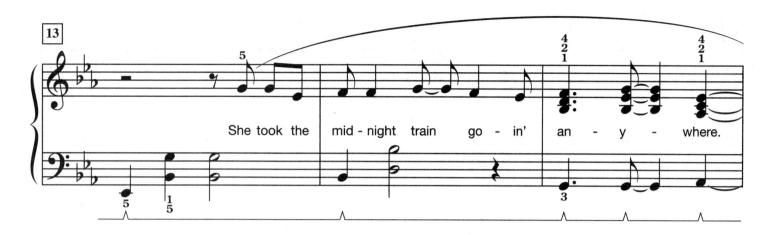

She took the mid - night train go - in' an - y - where.

Just a cit - y boy,

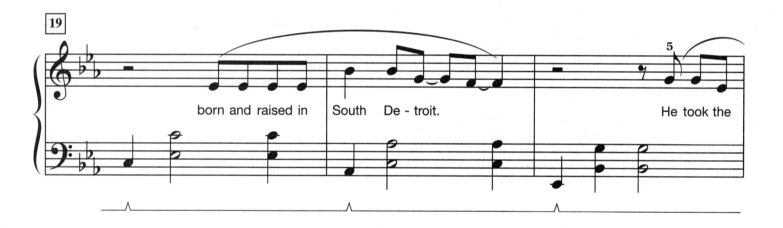

born and raised in South De - troit. He took the

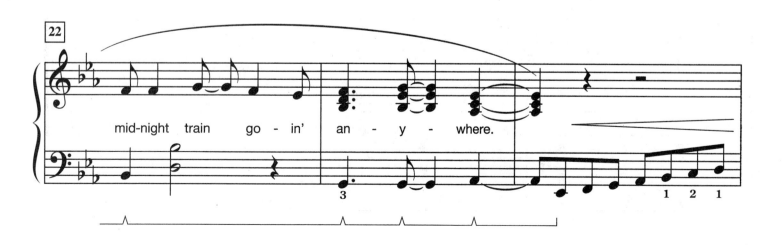

mid-night train go - in' an - y - where.

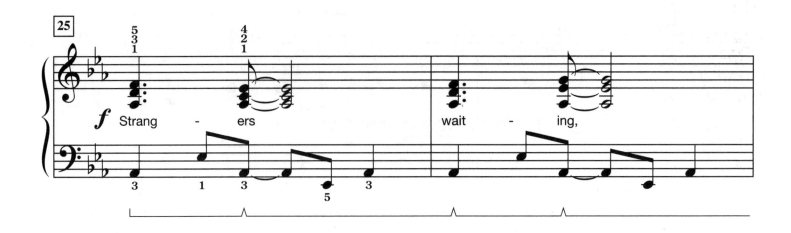

Strang - ers   wait -   ing,

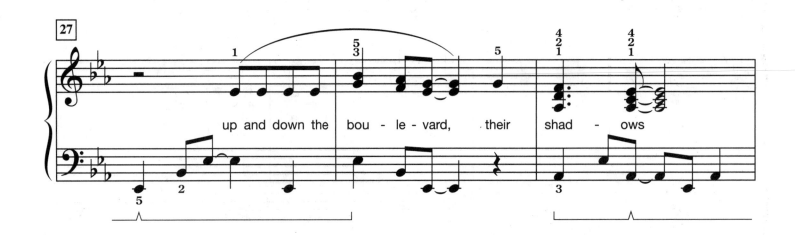

up and down the   bou - le - vard,   their   shad - ows

search - ing   in the   night.